'TWAS THE NIGHT THEY'LL REMEMBER

By Chuck Porretto
Illustrated by JD Crowe

**Dedicated to my mother Carol,
who taught me how to love,
and to my father Charlie,
who taught me how to laugh.**

32 South Section Street
Fairhope, AL 36532
www.pageandpalette.com

THE MOTHER OF ALL IRON BOWLS

'TWAS THE NIGHT AFTER AUBURN
AND ALL THROUGH THE LAND,
NOT A "ROLL TIDE" WAS UTTERED
BY A CRIMSON TIDE FAN.

THEY USED TO BE BOISTEROUS,
THEY USED TO BE LOUD,
THEY USED TO BE BOASTFUL,
AND COCKY AND PROUD.

AND SO, THE NATIONAL CHAMPIONSHIP TROPHY IS BACK WHERE IT BELONGS
SHORE IS PURTY
CAN WE PET IT?
WAL★MART
JDCROWE PRESS-REGISTER
CROWETOONS.com
http://blog.al.com/jdcrowe

BUT THEY LOST ALL THEIR SWAGGER,
THEY LOST ALL THEIR SWING.
FOR ONE LITTLE SECOND
HAD CHANGED EVERYTHING.

THE SCORE IT WAS EVEN.
THE CLOCK HAD RUN DRY.
WHEN NICHOLAS SABAN
THEN STARTED TO CRY.

HE DEMANDED A SECOND
BE PUT ON THE CLOCK.
THE WORSE THAT COULD HAPPEN?
A MISS?
OR A BLOCK?

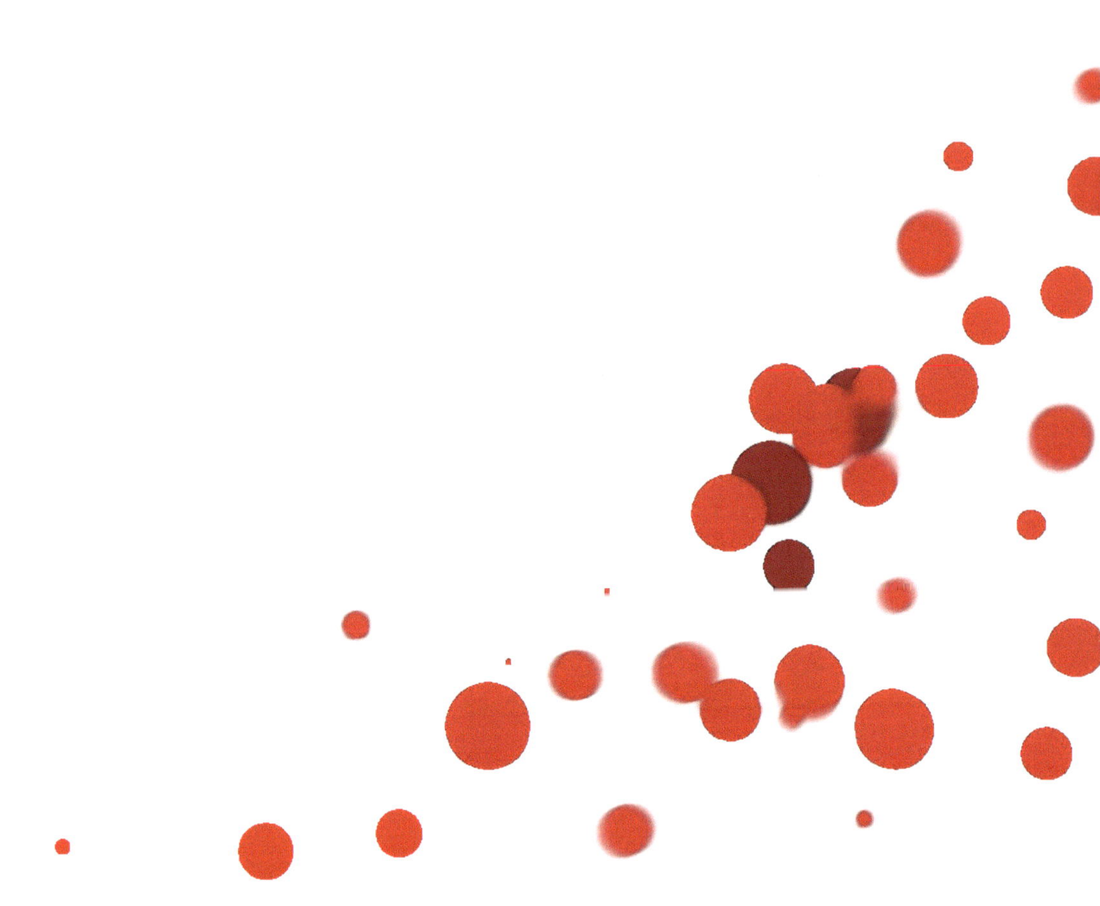

SECOND
JDC

BUT FATE IT IS FICKLE,
AND GREED HAS A PRICE,
AND WHAT HAPPENED NEXT
JUST WASN'T TOO NICE.

FAREWELL, TOOMER'S OAKS
AL.com

THE PREVIOUS KICKS,
WIDE LEFT AND WIDE RIGHT.
SO HE PUT IN A ROOKIE,
'TWAS NOT VERY BRIGHT.

POP
FIZZLE

THE KICK WAS A BOOMER
OF 56 YARDS,
BUT THE EXTRA YARD NEEDED
WAS NOT IN THE CARDS.

AND BACK IN THE END ZONE
A LONE TIGER STOOD.
HE CAUGHT THAT OL' FOOTBALL,
HE CAUGHT IT REAL GOOD.

JDC

HE STARTED TO RUN
AND HE HEARD THE CHEERS GROW.
THE CRIMSON TIDE OFFENSE?
TOO **FAT** AND TOO **SL**ow.

ONE HUNDRED AND NINE
HE RAN FOR A SCORE.
IF NEEDED HE COULD HAVE
RUN ONE HUNDRED MORE.

GOT A SECOND? I HAVE something

WANNA RUN BY YOU...
JDC

THE CROWD IT ERUPTED
WHILE STORMING THE FIELD.
THE CRIMSON TIDE'S SEASON
WAS SETTLED AND SEALED.

A CRY OF "WAR EAGLE"
SOON ECHOED THE PLAIN.
NICK SABAN'S EXPRESSION
WAS ONE OF PURE PAIN.

WAR EAGLE

AND UP IN OHIO
THEY SHOUTED "GO BUCKS",
FOR IT GAVE HOPE TO ALL
WELL, EXCEPT FOR THE DUCKS.

AND IN TUSCALOOSA
YOU COULD HEAR A PIN DROP.
AND IN TALLAHASSEE
A TOMAHAWK CHOP.

"All plant life must die."

FOR THE NIGHT AFTER AUBURN
THE TIDE IS NOW THROUGH.
THE NEW BOSS IN TOWN
WEARS ORANGE AND BLUE.

The lone Tiger was Chris Davis who many claim will go down in history as the man who starred in the most exciting finish in college football!

And major raves for Rod Bramblett, Auburn's radio broadcaster, who offered up an enthusiastic, red-hot play-by-play that sports fans all over America will never forget.

"Davis is gonna run it all the way back!" Bramblett told listeners as Davis crossed midfield Saturday inside Jordan-Hare Stadium "Auburn is gonna win the football game! Auburn is gonna win the football game! He ran the missed field goal back! He ran it back 109 yards!

They're not gonna keep 'em off the field tonight! HOLY COW!

Oh my God! Auburn wins! Auburn has won the Iron Bowl in the most unbelievable fashion you will ever see! I cannot believe it! 34-28! And we thought a Miracle in Jordan-Hare was amazing! Oh my Lord in Heaven!"

WAR EAGLE
RISING

AUBURN
2013 SEC CHAMPS

J.D. CROWE ALABAMA MEDIA GROUP

CPSIA information can be obtained
at www.ICGtesting.com
Printed in the USA
LVIW02n1414161213
365538LV00001BA/1